kokoro & moi

La collection design&designer est éditée par
PYRAMYD NTCV
15, rue de Turbigo
75002 Paris France

Tél. : 33 (0) 1 40 26 00 99
Fax : 33 (0) 1 40 26 00 79
www.pyramyd-editions.com

Direction éditoriale : Michel Chanaud, Céline Remechido
Suivi éditorial : Émilie Lamy assistée de Clémence Thomas
Traduction : Martine Desoille
Correction : Dominique Védy, Paul Jones
Conception graphique du livre : Anna Tunick
Conception graphique de la couverture : Pyramyd NTCV
Conception graphique de la collection : Super Cinq

ISBN : 978-2-35017-131-9
ISSN : 1636-8150
Dépôt légal : juillet 2008

Imprimé en Italie par Eurografica

kokoro & moi

préfacé par jenna sutela

PYRAMYD

Au nombre des prouesses réalisées par l'agence Kokoro & Moi au cours de ses huit années d'existence, citons, en tout premier lieu, celle d'avoir débuté dans des conditions plus que spartiates.

En 2001, quand Teemu Suviala et Antti Hinkula s'installent à Iso Rooberinkatu au cœur d'Helsinki, ils ne possèdent en tout et pour tout qu'un PowerBook G3, deux cartons de fournitures et quinze litres de peinture rouge. De ce studio plus que modeste, le tandem va faire ce qu'il estime avoir été sa plus belle création. C'est là que les deux compères frais émoulus de l'institut de design Lahti, où ils ont lié connaissance alors qu'ils étudiaient le Nombre d'or et la théorie des couleurs, vont commencer à honorer les premières commandes d'une clientèle internationale.

Autre exploit digne d'être mentionné ici, l'installation de l'équipe dans les locaux qu'elle occupe actuellement. En 2003, en raison d'une prolifération anarchique d'ordinateurs et de pots de peinture, Kokoro & Moi décide de déménager à Pursimiehenkatu. D'autres collaborateurs, stagiaires originaires de Suède et de Suisse, viennent alors grossir les rangs du studio qui compte déjà quelques employés et associés réguliers. Selon leur dernière recrue, issue d'une agence de publicité traditionnelle,

If the design consultancy Kokoro & Moi were to compile a record book of the most memorable moments in their eight-year history to date, the book would have to begin by nominating their most ascetic studio set-up. When Teemu Suviala and Antti Hinkula set up their first studio in Iso Roobertinkatu in the heart of Helsinki in 2001, their inventory consisted of one PowerBook G3, two cardboard boxes and fifteen litres of red paint. The duo set about turning this most humble of beginnings into what they regard as their finest creation. It was here that they started to work for their first international clients right after finishing their studies at the Lahti Institute of Design, where they had met amid the hue circles and golden canons so familiar to students of classical graphic design.

Best runner-up on the set-up scene would be their second studio, which is also their current one. Relocating to Pursimiehenkatu in 2003 resulted in a proliferation of both desktops and colours. In addition to new employees and local partners, trainees mostly from Sweden and Switzerland have dropped in with their laptops every so often. Coming from a big and more traditional design studio, their latest recruit describes the office

il souffle sur le studio comme un vent d'aventure. Elle explique que ce qu'elle apprécie tout particulièrement chez Kokoro & Moi, c'est de pouvoir sortir de temps à autre des sentiers battus.

En l'espace de quelques années, l'agence s'est trouvée submergée par les commandes tant dans le domaine de la création graphique et de produits que dans le Web design, le design spatial et conceptuel. Parmi les propositions les plus insolites jamais reçues par l'agence figure celle d'une firme iranienne leur proposant une fusion entre leurs deux sociétés. But de l'opération ? Exporter des dattes à bas coût vers la Finlande pour que l'agence (providentiellement nommée Syrup Helsinki à l'époque) puisse fabriquer du sirop. Dans un tout autre style, citons la commande la plus succincte qui leur fût jamais adressée. À peu près à la même époque, en 2002, la maison de disques japonaise Escalator Records leur envoie un e-mail signé Yugo Katayama : « Durée du titre environ trois minutes, simple/funky/punk/drôle/cool, date limite : lundi 24 janvier. » Armée de ces quelques indications et d'un échantillon sonore attaché en pièce jointe, l'agence va réaliser un vidéoclip pour Yukari Fresh, l'un des chanteurs préférés de Teemu à l'époque où il était étudiant à Lahti.

atmosphere as adventurous. She revels in the fact that at Kokoro & Moi stepping out of line now and again is actually encouraged.

Over the years, the office mailboxes have been inundated with commissions ranging from graphic to product design, from digital media to spatial work and concepts. Among the company's nominations for the strangest business proposals would be a query that surfaced in September 2002, when they were contacted by an Iranian company which proposed an alliance between the two businesses. Their plan? To export cut-price dates to Finland so that the office (invitingly dubbed Syrup Helsinki at that time) could produce syrup. In contrast, the most straightforward commission was received around the same time from the Japanese record company Escalator Records when Yugo Katayama sent a concise brief for a music video by email saying nothing more than the following: "Around 3 minutes song, cheap/funky/punk/funny/cool, deadline: Jan 24 Monday." Armed with these succinct guidelines and a sound clip attached to the email, the office made a music video for Yukari Fresh, one of Teemu's favourite artists from his and Antti's student days in Lahti.

Mais si variées que soient les commandes qui leur sont adressées, celles-ci ne coïncident pas toujours avec leurs aspirations. Ce que Kokoro & Moi aime avant tout, c'est relever des défis. Et le fait est que leur *leitmotiv* « créativité encore et toujours » et leur approche interdisciplinaire leur permettent de mélanger les genres avec bonheur.

Les trajets en ville sont, affirment-ils, leur meilleur outil de travail ainsi qu'une source d'inspiration. C'est pour cette raison que Kokoro & Moi préfère emprunter les itinéraires les plus longs pour se rendre au travail. Ils aiment aller se perdre dans le labyrinthe orange des baraques à café de la place du marché, située au sud d'Helsinki, et flâner à l'aube dans les allées paisibles du parc Kaivopuisto. À vélo, il ne faut que huit minutes à Teemu pour se rendre au studio, record battu récemment en vingt-cinq secondes chrono par Antti.

Quand ils ne sont pas en vadrouille, c'est dans l'un des troquets proches du studio (jadis quartier des marins-pêcheurs) que Kokoro & Moi cherche l'inspiration autour d'un copieux déjeuner arrosé d'une bonne dose de musique. Le tandem compare son travail à celui de musiciens, témoins leurs toutes

Kokoro & Moi's commissions are diverse to say the least, and their dream assignment is always a bit different from the ones they have in hand at any given moment. The office positively welcomes challenges, and with creative thinking as their leitmotif they have the ability to work across disciplines. They regard commuting as the best design tool as it is a good way to come up with new ideas. For this reason, Kokoro & Moi likes to take the longer route to work. The longest meanderings have been made on foot through the orange coffee stalls in the market place on the southern coast of Helsinki and around the tranquil Kaivopuisto park at daybreak. Travelling by bike, it only takes eight minutes for Teemu to get to work from home, while Antti has recently set a new record of 25 seconds.

When not in transit, a hearty lunch served in one of the eateries near the office (an area formerly populated by seafarers) feeds Kokoro & Moi's inspiration, seasoned with a large helping of music on the side. The duo sometimes compare their work to music-making. This is most apparent in their early creations for the Koneisto Festival for electronic music, in which their designs clearly bear the hallmark of the samples, rhythms and

premières créations pour le festival de musique électronique de Koneisto qui font clairement écho au rythme et aux mélodies des créations sonores. Kokoro & Moi a un penchant certain pour l'insolite. D'après eux, c'est en portant un regard décalé sur le monde qu'on arrive à des résultats réellement innovants et intéressants. Toutefois, il arrive qu'un projet au départ extraordinairement compliqué évolue au fil du temps vers quelque chose de plus épuré. Et, inversement, une idée toute simple peut se mettre à germer après qu'on a quitté le bureau et prendre des proportions inattendues. Ils citent volontiers, comme exemple, la campagne de 2008 pour Bon Bon Kakku, une entreprise de design textile en ligne. Le modèle conçu dans une étoffe aux couleurs chatoyantes, qui a servi à faire la promo du site, a été repris par un journal arabe pour illustrer un article sur l'austère burkha. Cette anecdote mérite d'être mentionnée dans la liste des records, même s'il s'agit davantage d'un concours de circonstances que d'une démarche intentionnelle de la part des intéressés.

Kokoro & Moi croit très fort en l'intuition. L'agence a adopté son nouveau nom après que l'enseigne d'un restaurant de Bergen a attiré l'attention du tandem. Ledit restaurant, Bølgen & Moi, tenait son

melodies. Mirroring their taste in music, Kokoro & Moi has a penchant for the curious and the extraordinary when it comes to design patterns. Looking at things sideways can lead to something new and exciting, according to the duo. On the other hand, in many cases projects start from the most complicated ideas and gradually evolve towards something more simple. Yet, conversely, ideas can also be elevated to another level of complexity after leaving the office. A case in point is the 2008 campaign for Bon Bon Kakku, a web-based textile design service. A model swathed in bright-coloured fabric for the promotional photo shoot was later spotted in the Arabian press in an article dealing with more sombre burkha clothing. This incident definitely deserves a mention in their book of records as one of the most multidimensional designs, even if it was only by association.

Kokoro & Moi trusts its intuition. The office acquired its new name after the owners spotted a restaurant sign to their liking in Bergen. It just so happens that the restaurant, Bølgen & Moi, was named after two Norwegian super chefs. Foregoing the more traditional Suviala & Hinkula, Teemu and Antti decided to call their office

nom des deux grands chefs norvégiens. Passant outre le traditionnel Suviala & Hinkula, Teemu et Antti décidèrent de baptiser leur agence Kokoro & Moi – « kokoro » signifiant « esprit », « cœur » et « âme » en japonais et « moi » évoquant non seulement le chef cuisinier Trond Moi, mais aussi signifiant en finnois « salut » et « moi » en français. L'ambiguïté du nom se retrouve dans la philosophie fondatrice du studio pour qui 1 + 1 = 3.

La palme d'or dans la catégorie élément graphique revient aux diagonales utilisées par l'agence pour créer des logos d'entreprises. Bien que ses collègues disent de Teemu qu'il ressemble à un cercle rouge, la symétrie parfaite n'a fait que récemment son apparition dans les créations de Kokoro & Moi. Antti aime à décrire Kokoro comme un cercle et Moi comme une éclaboussure, dans la mesure où leurs illustrations offrent rarement des contours réguliers. À première vue, leurs créations donnent une impression d'aisance et de légèreté, mais sous la surface se cachent un gros travail conceptuel et une quantité de références culturelles, comme si nos deux compères cherchaient à repousser toujours plus loin leurs propres limites.

Kokoro & Moi – "kokoro" meaning "heart", "mind" and "soul" in Japanese and "moi" bringing to mind not only Trond Moi, but also "hello" in Finnish as well as "me" in French. The ambiguity of the name is reflected in the studio's intrinsic design principle, whereby 1 + 1 = 3.

The top award in the most distinctive graphic element category has to go to the diagonals that the office has used in various brand identities. Even though colleagues say that Teemu can be compared to a red circle, the perfectly symmetrical shape has only recently made an appearance in Kokoro & Moi's work. Antti likes to describe Kokoro as a circle and Moi as a splash, since not all their designs have such neat edges. At first glance their work looks free and easy, but embedded within it is more than a hint of conceptual thinking and a number of cultural references. The boundaries always get pushed a bit further than expected.

The same diversity also applies to the way in which people react to their work. The studio's thought-provoking designs always seem to arouse a strong response one way or another. The most startling feedback was given by someone who sent an email a few years ago saying that they wanted to set off a bomb in the duo's office

Cette diversité se reflète dans la façon dont le public réagit à leurs œuvres. Leurs créations invitent le public à s'interroger, provoquant parfois des réactions violentes chez certains. La plus orageuse fut celle d'un internaute qui, révolté par le contenu de leur site Web, menaça de faire sauter leur agence. Cependant, la plupart de leurs clients adorent « les garçons de Kokoro & Moi », comme en témoigne cette femme qui fut tellement touchée de recevoir une facture rédigée à la main qu'elle s'en fût toute guillerette à la banque. Cela dit, la palme du plus grand fan de Teemu et Antti revient à leurs petites sœurs. Celle d'Antti joue les attachées de presse en recueillant religieusement tous les articles de journaux faisant référence au studio. Sa quête tous azimuts l'amène parfois à faire de curieuses trouvailles, comme cette fabrique de faux tee-shirts Kokoro & Moi basée en Thaïlande.

Teemu et Antti croient à leur bonne étoile et ne se lassent pas de raconter la fois où, en 2006, ayant commandé une pizza pour le déjeuner, ils ont découvert que la boîte en contenait deux. Si l'incident a tellement frappé l'imagination du tandem, c'est parce qu'il s'accorde parfaitement avec son état d'esprit décalé : simple/funky/punk/drôle/cool.

after they had seen one of the designs in their web portfolio. Yet most of the clients really love "the boys at Kokoro & Moi". One lady said that she was so touched to receive an invoice with a handwritten address on it that she smiled all the way to the bank. Still, the nomination for the most dedicated fans must go to Teemu's and Antti's little sisters. Antti's sister is a veritable PR bot with all her newspaper and magazine clippings and online odysseys for anything to do with the office. Her various quests have even unearthed the odd surprise, like the time she discovered fake Kokoro & Moi T-shirts in Thailand.

Teemu and Antti never underestimate the power of serendipity. The owners often recount the story of their luckiest day in 2006 when they bought a pizza for lunch and discovered that the box actually contained not one, but two pizzas. The incident resonates with the duo because it seemed to tie in so well with their philosophy of thinking outside the box – and designing something cheap/funky/punk/funny/cool, while on the move.

Au cours de ses huit années d'existence, l'intrépide duo a travaillé pour les clients aux sensibilités les plus diverses. Toujours à l'affût de nouveauté et d'aventure, Kokoro & Moi ne cesse de nous épater.

Jenna Sutela
Journaliste et graphiste

During its intrepid eight-year history, the office has embraced a variety of clients, tasks, design solutions and playlists. In its exploration of the new and the different, the best of Kokoro & Moi just keeps on getting better all the time.

Jenna Sutela
Journalist and designer

PAGES 12 À 17 :
IDENTITÉ DE LA MARQUE
BON BON KAKKU
LOGO, PHOTO PROMOTIONNELLE,
SITE INTERNET *(WWW.BONBONKAKKU.COM)*
ILLUSTRATION POUR TISSU
ET SAC DE COUCHAGE
CLIENT : BON BON KAKKU /
VALLILA INTERIOR
FINLANDE, 2008

PAGES 12 TO 17:
BON BON KAKKU IDENTITY
LOGOTYPE, PROMOTIONAL PHOTO,
WEBSITE *(WWW.BONBONKAKKU.COM)*
FABRIC DESIGN AND SLEEPING BAGS
CLIENT: BON BON KAKKU /
VALLILA INTERIOR
FINLAND, 2008

About
Shop
Score / Submit
My Account
Home

0 items in your shopping cart **Checkout**

R FABULOUS FABRICS OR DESIGN YOUR OWN AND GET FAMOUS.

Latest 3 fabrics in the shop!

See More >>

Nada Go-Go
by Nada Go-Go

Chisulo
by Nada Go-Go

Rapatunii
by Nada Go-Go

Latest 6 designs in the vote!

See More >>

Hotel Carton
by Kokoro & Moi

Guran Guran
by Kokoro & Moi

MD-DAD
by Kokoro & Moi

Kokoro & Moi & Bico
by Kokoro & Moi

New Plus
by Kokoro & Moi

RainbowbirdG2
by Paola

Bon Bon Kakku Broadcast

Grand Opening of Store!

Bon Bon Kakku opened! This is the place to set your inner designer free! Design your very own fabric print, or five if you get really creative! You can follow up your success in viewer polling and even have your creation on sale on net store.
Read more
(2008-03-18 16:31:42)

In Paris with Paola!

The founder of the Finnish brand IVANAhelsinki Paola Suhonen was the first Finnish fashion designer to be invited to the main shows of Paris's Fashion Week. Paola has also designed Bon Bon Kakku fabric...
Read more
(2008-03-13 14:34:56)

© 2008 Vallila Interior. All designs copyright by owner.   Privacy / Terms of use / Contact / Help / Press

VALLILA

14

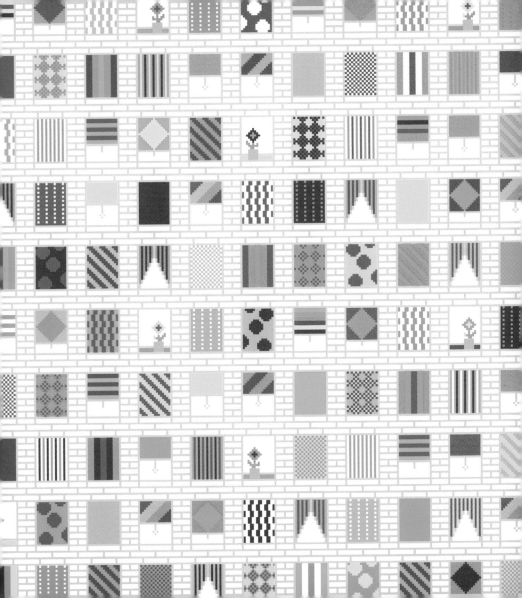

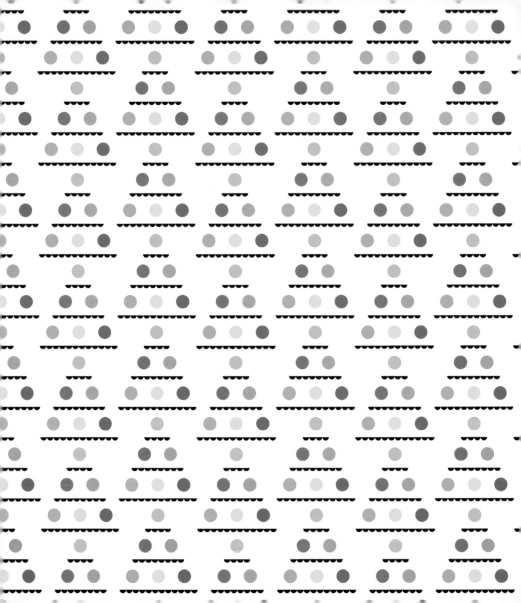

LOGOTYPES
CLIENTS : SYRUP, INC. ; BLÄK NIGHTCLUB ;
BANQUET ; BNQT.COM, INC.
ET BIKINI WAX CLUB
2004-2007

LOGOTYPES
CLIENT: SYRUP, INC.; BLÄK NIGHTCLUB;
BANQUET; BNQT.COM, INC.
AND BIKINI WAX CLUB
2004-2007

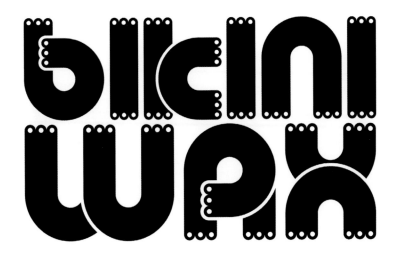

French Fork

Balbo

A la scousarov

Friendly Mutton Chops

Mutton Chops

Van Dyke

Hollywoodian

Handlebar and Chin Puff

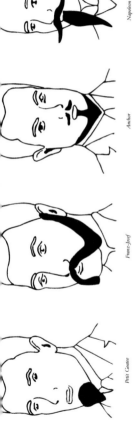

AFFICHE
CLIENT : BIKINI WAX CLUB
FINLANDE, 2004

POSTER
CLIENT: BIKINI WAX CLUB
FINLAND, 2004

KANSALLISTEATTERI

****

Hella Wuolijoki /

NISKAVUOREN NUORI EMÄNTÄ

****

ensi-ilta 17.12.04 /
Suuri näyttämö

****

ohjaus /
Juha Lehtola

koreografia /
Matti Paloniemi

musiikki /
Maria Kalaniemi

lavastus ja puvut /
Kristiina Saha

****

rooleissa /
Wanda Dubiel, Marjukka Halttunen, Olli Ikonen,
Markku Maalismaa, Minttu Mustakallio, Heikki
Nousiainen, Anna Paavilainen (Teak), Ilja
Peltonen, Seri Puumalainen, Katja Salminen,
Hanna Korhonen, Anna Paavilainen, Sami Paasila,
Reetta Pirhonen, Timo Saari

****

www.kansallisteatteri.fi

AFFICHE POUR LE FINNISH
NATIONAL THEATRE
FINLANDE, 2004

POSTER FOR THE FINNISH
NATIONAL THEATRE
FINLAND, 2004

PAGES SUIVANTES :
ILLUSTRATION DE PRESSE
CLIENT : IMAGE PUBLISHING
FINLANDE, 2005

NEXT PAGES:
EDITORIAL ILLUSTRATION
CLIENT: IMAGE PUBLISHING
FINLAND, 2005

VARIOUS PROMOTIONAL MATERIAL
FOR IITTALA 125th ANNIVERSARY
FINLAND, 2006

DIVERS SUPPORTS PROMOTIONNELS
POUR LE 125e ANNIVERSAIRE
DE LA MARQUE IITTALA
FINLANDE, 2006

LOGOTYPES
CLIENTS: KOSMOS AND LOUDER
FINLAND, 2003 AND 2007

LOGOTYPES
CLIENTS : KOSMOS ET LOUDER
FINLANDE, 2003 ET 2007

iittala

Hot Music for Cool Design.

Iittala's 125th anniversary

featuring:

Vilunki3000
T.A.Kaukolampi
Jori Hulkkonen
Esko Routamaa

Grandpeople

AFFICHE POUR LE CONCOURS
« YOUNG DESIGNERS OF THE YEAR »
CLIENT : DESIGN FORUM FINLAND
FINLANDE, 2005

POSTER FOR THE "YOUNG DESIGNERS
OF THE YEAR" CONTEST
CLIENT: DESIGN FORUM FINLAND
FINLAND, 2005

PORTRAIT DES MEMBRES
DE GRANDPEOPLE
CLIENT : WWP/IDN
ROYAUME-UNI, HONGKONG, 2007

GRANDPEOPLE MEMBERS PORTRAIT
CLIENT: WWP/IDN
UK, HONG KONG, 2007

PORTANT POUR ENCENS
CLIENT : LISN / SHOYEIDO CORP.
JAPON, 2007

INCENSE HOLDERS
CLIENT: LISN / SHOYEIDO CORP.
JAPAN, 2007

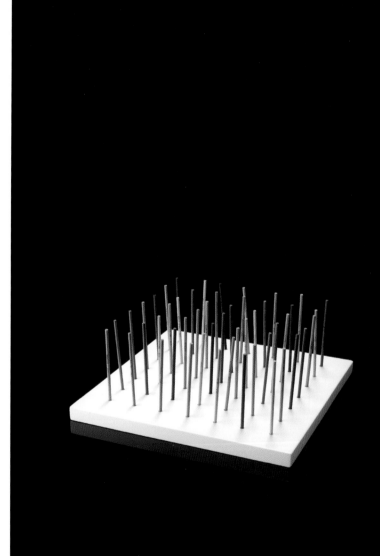

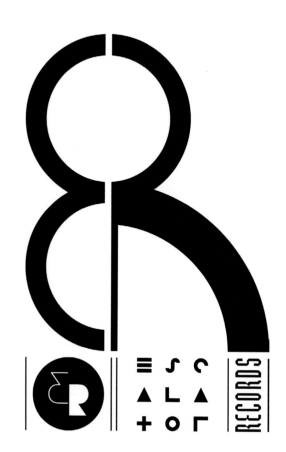

PAGES 33 À 35:
DESIGN OF THE *WE ARE ESCALATOR RECORDS* COMPILATIONS
CLIENT: ESCALATOR RECORDS
JAPAN, 2003-2006

PAGES 33 À 35 :
POCHETTES DES COMPILATIONS *WE ARE ESCALATOR RECORDS*
CLIENT : ESCALATOR RECORDS
JAPON, 2003-2006

LOGOTYPE
CLIENT: ESCALATOR RECORDS
JAPAN, 2006

LOGOTYPE
CLIENT : ESCALATOR RECORDS
JAPON, 2006

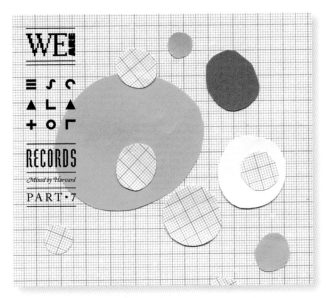

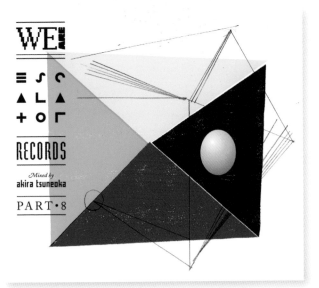

DESIGN OF THE *WE ARE ESCALATOR RECORDS* COMPILATIONS
CLIENT: ESCALATOR RECORDS
JAPAN, 2008

POCHETTES DES COMPILATIONS *WE ARE ESCALATOR RECORDS*
CLIENT : ESCALATOR RECORDS
JAPON, 2008

DEATH TO MUSIC BIZ ILLUSTRATION
CLIENT: ESCALATOR RECORDS
JAPAN, 2005

ILLUSTRATION *DEATH TO MUSIC BIZ*
CLIENT : ESCALATOR RECORDS
JAPON, 2005

GOLDHAMMER IDENTITY
PRINT DESIGN
CLIENT: KARHU SPORTING GOODS
FINLAND, 2006

IDENTITÉ DE LA MARQUE GOLDHAMMER
IMPRESSION SUR TEXTILE
CLIENT : KARHU SPORTING GOODS
FINLANDE, 2006

UNTITLED
PRINT DESIGN
CLIENT: ESCALATOR RECORDS
JAPAN, 2006

SANS TITRE
IMPRESSION SUR TEXTILE
CLIENT : ESCALATOR RECORDS
JAPON, 2006

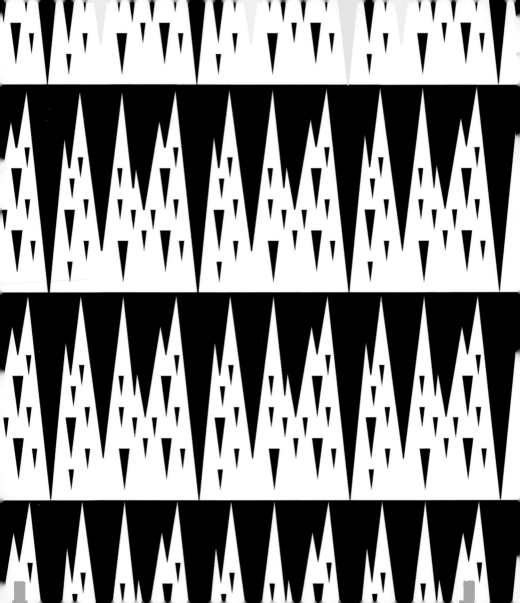

POSTER FOR THE JIM & JILL
CLOTHES BRAND
FINLAND, 2005

AFFICHE POUR LA MARQUE
DE VÊTEMENTS JIM & JILL
FINLANDE, 2005

ICE COLD
PRINT DESIGN
CLIENT : JIM & JILL
FINLAND, 2008

FROID GLACIAL
IMPRESSION SUR TEXTILE
CLIENT : JIM & JILL
FINLANDE, 2008

POSTER FOR THE SUMMER SALES
CLIENT: JIM & JILL
FINLAND, 2007

AFFICHE POUR LES SOLDES D'ÉTÉ
CLIENT : JIM & JILL
FINLANDE, 2007

THE WORLD IS LOOKING AT ME AND IT LIKES WHAT IT SEES

CONCEPTION GRAPHIQUE
DE LA POCHETTE DE L'ALBUM
TELEMACHO DU GROUPE
MR VELCRO FASTENER
FINLANDE, 2006

DESIGN OF THE *TELEMACHO* ALBUM
OF THE MR VELCRO FASTENER
BAND
FINLAND, 2006

SANS TITRE
ILLUSTRATION POUR
LE MAGAZINE *WAD*
FRANCE, 2007

UNTITLED
ILLUSTRATION FOR
WAD MAGAZINE
FRANCE, 2007

SYRUP — HELSINKI

FESTIVAL FOR ELECTRONIC MUSIC and ARTS

July 25th-27th, 2003 ∾ Kaapeli, Helsinki

Liput ennakkoon ∾ 1 päivä 37 euroa (pe tai la), 3 päivää 65 euroa
Liput portilla ∾ 1 päivä 40 euroa (pe tai la), 3 päivää 70 euroa
Ennakkomyynti ∾ Street Beat, Lifesaver, Mbar, Free Record Shop/s,
Lippupalvelu 0600 10800 (1 e/min+pvm) & www.lippupalvelu.fi,
Tiketti 0600 11616 (0,66 e/min+pvm) & www.tiketti.fi

www.koneisto.com

POSTER FOR THE "KONEISTO"
ELECTRONIC MUSIC FESTIVAL
FINLAND, 2003

AFFICHE POUR LE FESTIVAL
DE MUSIQUE ÉLECTRONIQUE
« KONEISTO »
FINLANDE, 2003

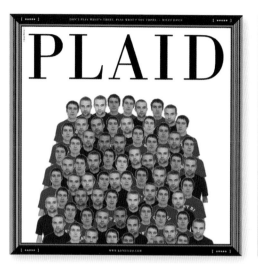

E L L E N

[Sprip Helsinki]

A L L I E N

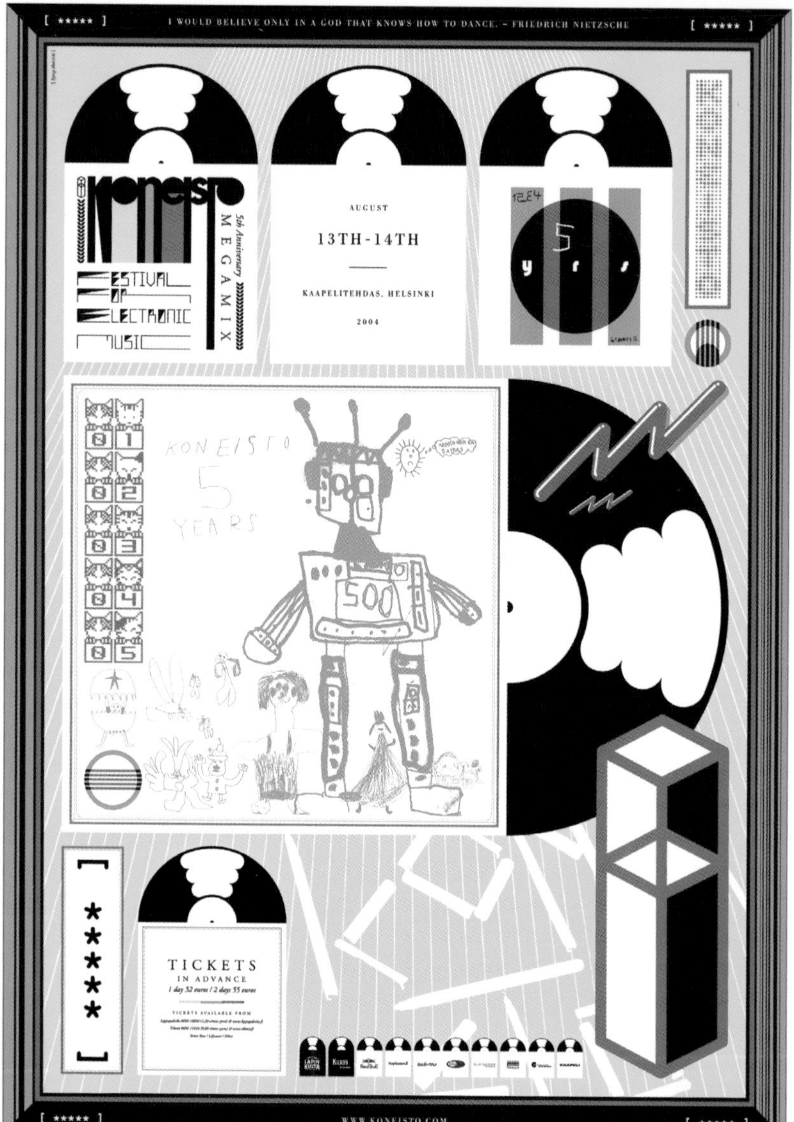

[*****]
I WOULD BELIEVE ONLY IN A GOD THAT KNOWS HOW TO DANCE. – FRIEDRICH NIETZSCHE
[*****]
KONEISTO
FESTIVAL OF ELECTRONIC MUSIC
5th Anniversary MEGAMIX
AUGUST
13TH-14TH
KAAPELITEHDAS, HELSINKI
2004
KONEISTO
5
YEARS
500
TICKETS
IN ADVANCE
1 day 32 euros / 2 days 55 euros
TICKETS AVAILABLE FROM
[*****]
WWW.KONEISTO.COM
[*****]

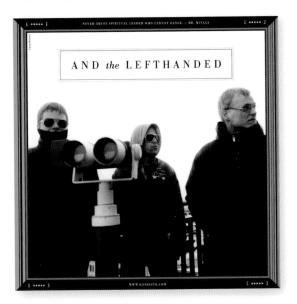

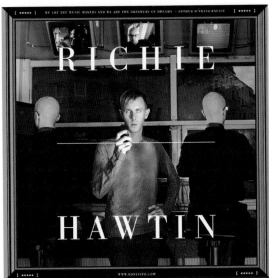

PAGES 48 À 53 :
IDENTITÉ DU FESTIVAL DE MUSIQUE
ELECTRONIQUE « KONEISTO »
DIVERS SUPPORTS PROMOTIONNELS
FINLANDE, 2004, 2002

PAGES 48 TO 53:
POSTER FOR THE "KONEISTO"
ELECTRONIC MUSIC FESTIVAL
VARIOUS PROMOTIONAL MATERIAL
FINLAND, 2004, 2002

KONEISTO

über

KONEISTO 2002

Say yes to no.

Se on se feeling.

KONEISTO

KONEISTO.COM

Festival for electronic music and arts.
July 26th-28th. 2002. Helsinki. Finland.

Helsingin kaupungin
kulttuuriasiainkeskus

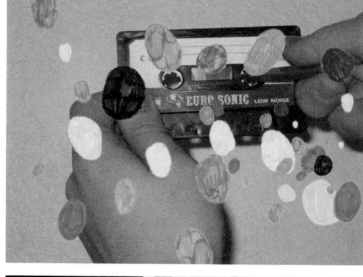

YKR PLYS TH GTR DRMS
VIDEO CLIP
CLIENT : YUKARI FRESH
JAPAN, 2005

PUBLICITÉ POUR LE LANCEMENT
DE LA TOYOTA AYGO
ROYAUME-UNI, 2005

ADVERTISEMENT FOR THE TOYOTA
AYGO LAUNCH CAMPAIGN
UK, 2005

YKR PLYS TH GTR DRMS
VIDEOCLIP
CLIENT : YUKARI FRESH
JAPON, 2005

YKR PLYS TH GTR DRMS
VIDEO CLIP
CLIENT : YUKARI FRESH
JAPON, 2005

PAGES 57 TO 59:
POSTERS FOR THE NADA GO-GO
BRAND SPRING-SUMMER COLLECTION
FINLAND, 2007

PAGES 57 À 59 :
AFFICHES POUR LA COLLECTION
PRINTEMPS-ÉTÉ DE LA MARQUE
NADA GO-GO
FINLANDE, 2007

MUOTOVALIOT
ILLUSTRATION FOR
MUOTO MAGAZINE
FINLAND, 2005

MUOTOVALIOT
ILLUSTRATION POUR
LE MAGAZINE MUOTO
FINLANDE, 2005

HIGH PRIORITY
ILLUSTRATION FOR
NEW YORK MAGAZINE
USA, 2006

HIGH PRIORITY
ILLUSTRATION POUR
LE NEW YORK MAGAZINE
ETATS-UNIS, 2006

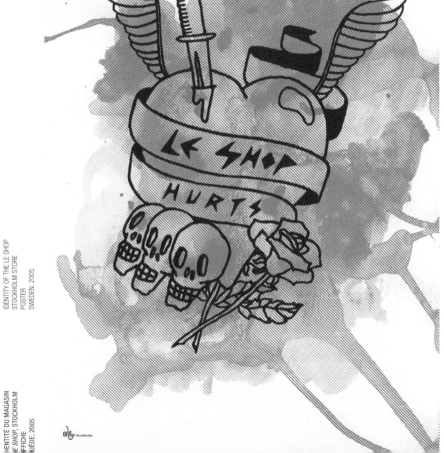

IDENTITY OF THE LE SHOP
STOCKHOLM STORE
POSTER
SWEDEN, 2005

ENTITÉ DU MAGASIN
E SHOP, STOCKHOLM
FFICHE
UÈDE, 2005

PïIa / HÄNNINEN

S/S 2008

IDENTITY OF THE PïIA
HÄNNINEN BRAND
POSTER
ITALY, 2008

IDENTITÉ DE LA MARQUE
PïIA HÄNNINEN
AFFICHE
ITALIE, 2008

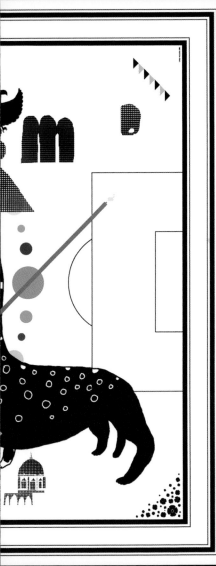

FEDE PER LA PALERMO
AFFICHE POUR LA VILLE
DE PALERME
ITALIE, 2006

FEDE PER LA PALERMO
POSTER FOR THE CITY
OF PALERMO
ITALY, 2006

THE CRASH

THE CRASH

IDENTITÉ DU GROUPE
THE CRASH
LOGOTYPES
FINLANDE, 2005-2006

IDENTITY OF THE CRASH BAND
LOGOTYPES
FINLAND, 2005-2006

CONCEPTION GRAPHIQUE
DE LA POCHETTE DE L'ALBUM
SELECTED SONGS 1999-2005
DU GROUPE THE CRASH
FINLANDE, 2005

DESIGN OF THE *SELECTED*
SONGS 1999-2005 ALBUM
OF THE CRASH BAND
FINLAND, 2005

THE CR▲SH

·SELECTED SONGS·
1999 — 2005

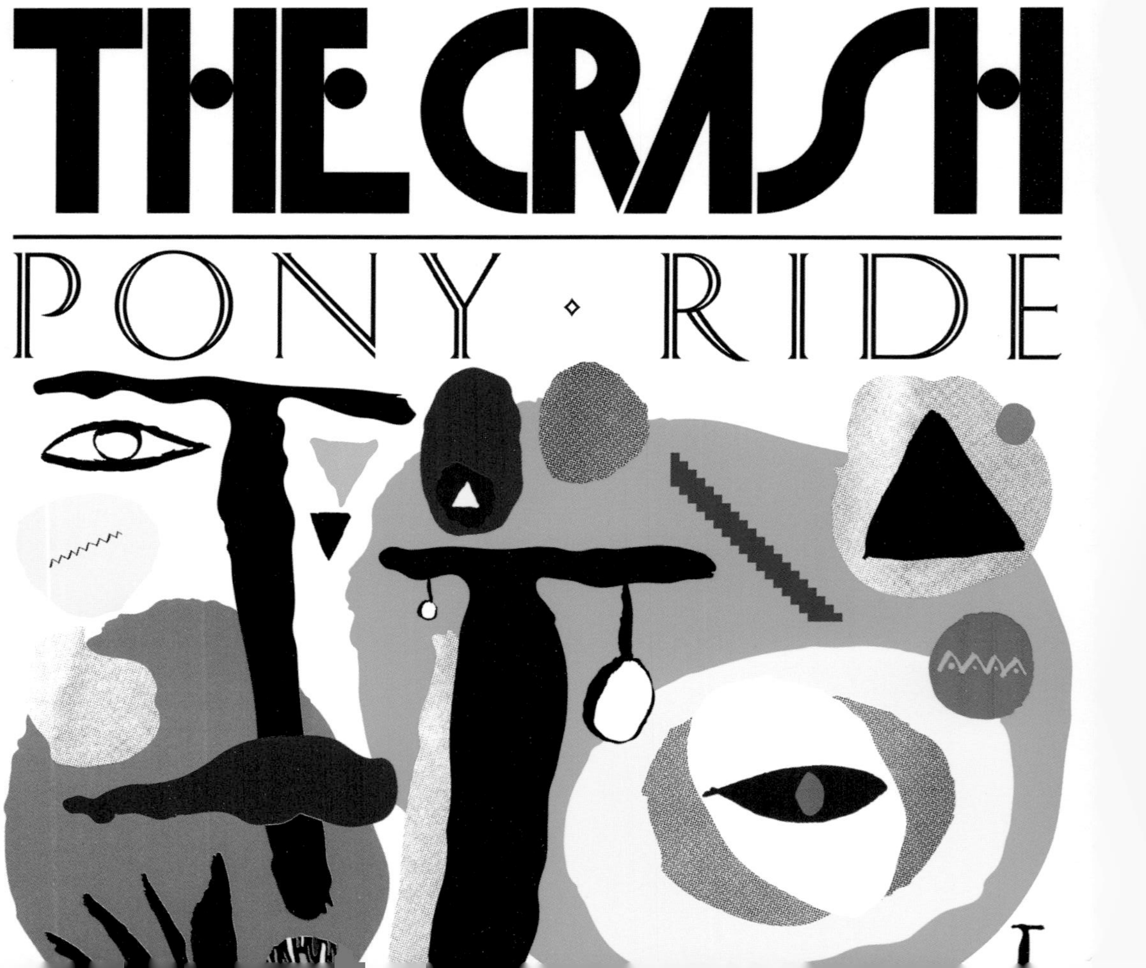
THE CRASH
PONY RIDE

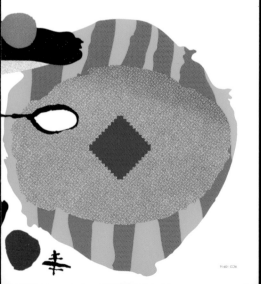

PONY RIDE
LIVRET / AFFICHE
CLIENT : THE CRASH
FINLANDE, 2006

PONY RIDE
BOOKLET/POSTER
CLIENT: THE CRASH
FINLAND, 2006

91601 CON

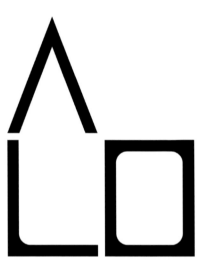

IDENTITÉ DU GROUPE I'DEES
LOGOTYPE
CLIENT : SONY MUSIC
FINLANDE, 2004

IDENTITY OF I'DEES BAND
LOGOTYPE
CLIENT: SONY MUSIC
FINLAND, 2004

IDENTITÉ DE JAIKU
LOGOTYPE
FINLANDE, 2006

JAIKU IDENTITY
LOGOTYPE
FINLAND, 2006

GLOBAL
LOCAL

Hel
sinki

IDENTITÉ DE LA MARQUE
GLOBAL LOCAL
LOGOTYPE
CLIENT : DESIGN FORUM FINLAND
FINLANDE, 2005

IDENTITY OF THE GLOBAL
LOCAL BRAND
LOGOTYPE
CLIENT: DESIGN FORUM FINLAND
FINLAND, 2005

PAGES SUIVANTES :
CRÉATION DU SITE INTERNET
DE PASSION PICTURES
WWW.PASSION-PICTURES.COM
ROYAUME-UNI, 2007

NEXT PAGES:
DESIGN OF PASSION PICTURES
WEBSITE
WWW.PASSION-PICTURES.COM
UK, 2007

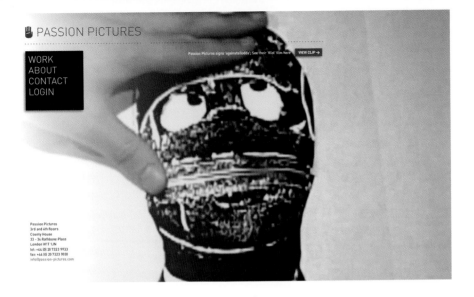

Huge & Mode — Seministit

"_____ is the new black" — *Wikipedia, 2007*

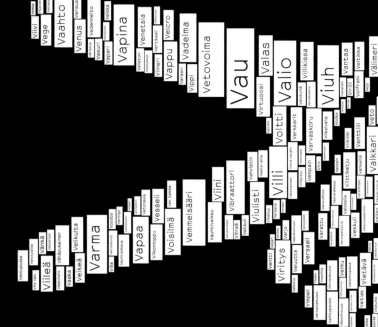

CAMPAGNE DE LANCEMENT
DU MAGAZINE V
PUBLICITÉ
CLIENT : SANOMA MAGAZINES
FINLANDE, 2006

V MAGAZINE LAUNCH CAMPAIGN
ADVERTISEMENT
CLIENT: SANOMA MAGAZINES
FINLAND, 2006

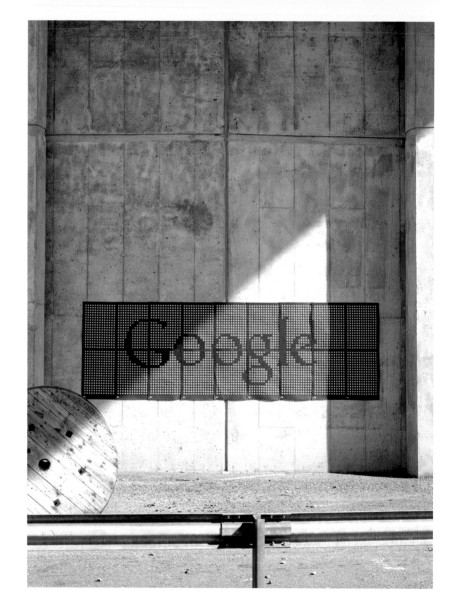

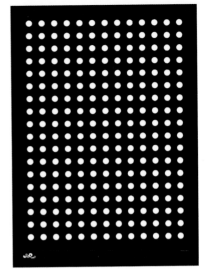

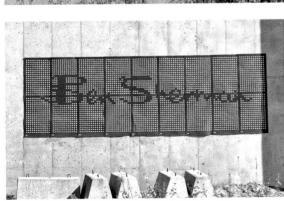

«234 DPP»
INSTALLATIONS D'AFFICHES
CLIENT : MAGAZINE *WAD*
FRANCE, 2006

"234 DPP"
POSTER INSTALLATIONS
CLIENT: *WAD* MAGAZINE
FRANCE, 2006

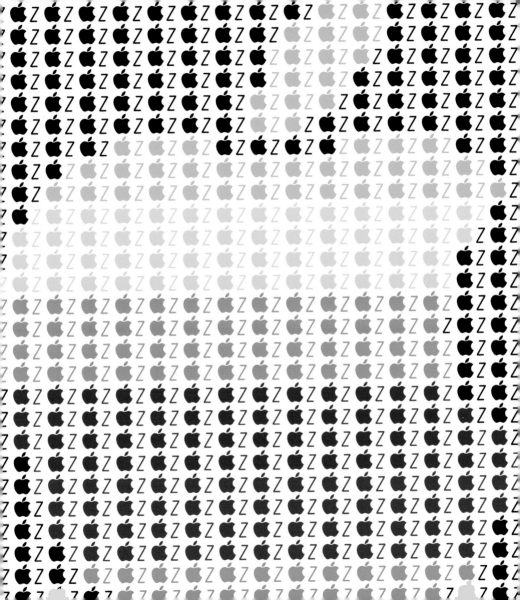

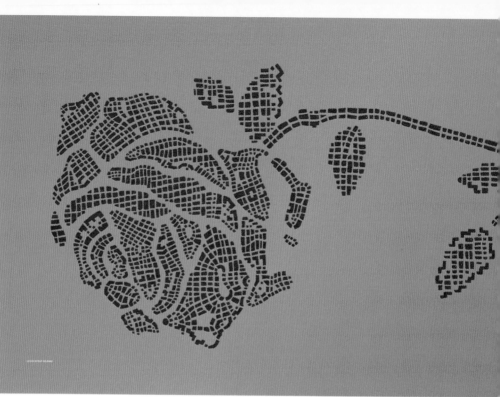

/ RAKENTAMISEN

RUUSU / 10 v. /

PAGE 82 :
« PENCIL »
ILLUSTRATION
CLIENT : MAGAZINE *METROPOLIS*
ÉTATS-UNIS, 2007

PAGE 82:
"PENCIL"
ILLUSTRATION
CLIENT: *METROPOLIS* MAGAZINE
USA, 2007

PAGE 83 :
« APPLE Z »
ILLUSTRATION
CLIENT : MAGAZINE *BULGARIA*
FINLANDE, 2005

PAGE 83:
"APPLE Z"
ILLUSTRATION
CLIENT: *BULGARIA* MAGAZINE
FINLAND, 2005

RAKENTAMISEN RUUSU
AFFICHE
CLIENT : VILLE D'HELSINKI
FINLANDE, 2006

RAKENTAMISEN RUUSU
POSTER
CLIENT: CITY OF HELSINKI
FINLAND, 2006

finndia

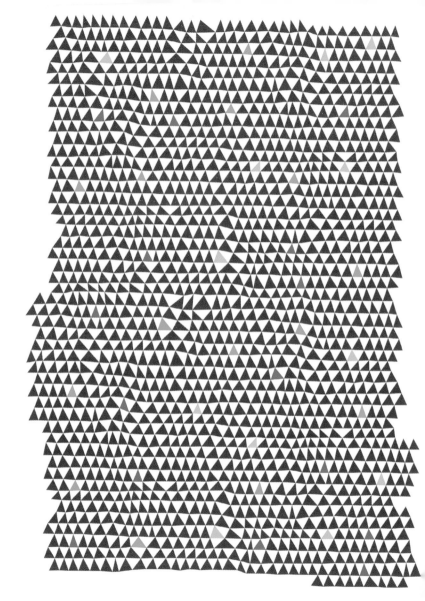

^ / Huippu / Design / Management

IDENTITÉ DE HUIPPU
DESIGN MANAGEMENT
MOTIF ET LOGOTYPE
FINLANDE, 2005

HUIPPU DESIGN MANAGEMENT
IDENTITY
PATTERN AND LOGOTYPE
FINLAND, 2005

PAGES SUIVANTES :
CARTE DE NOËL
ET SUPPORT PROMOTIONNEL
CLIENT : HUIPPU DESIGN MANAGEMENT
FINLANDE, 2005-2006

NEXT PAGES :
CHRISTMAS CARD AND LAUNCH
PROMOTIONAL MATERIAL
CLIENT: HUIPPU DESIGN MANAGEMENT
FINLAND, 2005-2006

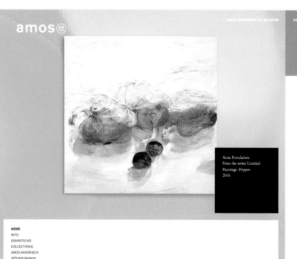

Anna Retulainen
From the series Untitled
Paintings: Pepper
2006

Museum is closed on Midsummer 22.–24.6.2007

New website

Amos Anderson Art Museum has renewed its website. The creative forces behind our fresh, stylish and playful new look is *Syrup Helsinki*. Big thanks!

New exhibition:
10.ax
Ten artists connected to the Åland Islands
15.6.–5.8.2007

Anna Retulainen and the Helsinki Festival

A feast of oil paintings both strong and sensitive by Anna Retulainen (b. 1969) at the Amos Anderson Art Museum 17.8.–16.9.2007. The exhibition is a part of *The Helsinki Festival*.

Museum Expansion

In 2007 Amos Anderson Art Museum will undergo refurbishment and expansion. Two exhibition floors will be added on the second and third levels. The entrance, ticket office, museum shop and cloakroom will be spruced up and streamlined. The new spaces will open to the public in the autumn.

Collaboration with the Finnish Art Foundations' Association

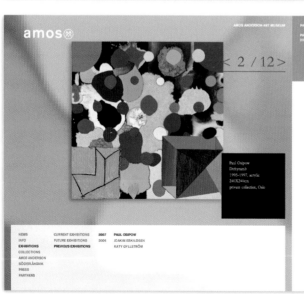

< 2 / 12 >

Paul Osipow
Dithyramb
1995–1997, acrylic
240x240cm
private collection, Oslo

Paul Osipow's paintings from 1994-2006 are on display at the Amos Anderson Art Museum 23.3.-13.5.2007. Paul Osipow (b.1939) entered the Finnish art scene in the mid-1960s and is perhaps best known as a painter of abstract, large-scale canvases utilizing geometrical forms. However, the paintings have gone through several transformations over the past decade.

The systems of abstract painting made way for playful spontaneity present in Pearl Paintings, a series painted in 1994 in New York. In contrast, Little (1999) is a vivid, lusciously executed abstract piece that changes guise from landscape to still life in the blink of an eye.

In 2002, Osipow's still life veered towards the tangible and figurative, with scrumptious paintings of pastries, peppers and sausages plucked from his neighbourhood in France or Italy to be pictured in the artist's studio. In 2004, themes originating from these countries include ruins, the past of the landscape, the ever-present temporal dimension of cultures.

Throughout the year 2006, Paul Osipow worked in Villa Lante in Rome, focusing on skulls, "human ruins".

Paul Osipow keeps pushing boundaries and possibilities; maintaining a dialogue between his actions and his medium, painting, continuously questioning himself. As soon as one line has been exhausted, he moves on to the next.

The exhibition catalogue includes interviews with Paul Osipow conducted by Petr Rehor (2006) and Jan Svenungsson (2004), as well as greetings from fellow artists Tor Arne, Juhana Blomstedt and Matti Kujasalo.

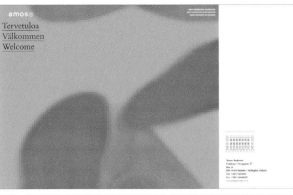

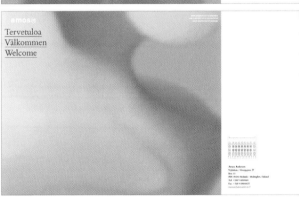

SITE INTERNET DU MUSÉE
AMOS ANDERSON
WWW.AMOSANDERSON.FI
HELSINKI, 2007

WEBSITE OF AMOS ANDERSON
ART MUSEUM
WWW.AMOSANDERSON.FI
HELSINKI, 2007

[LIBERTÉ D'EXPRESSION]
AFFICHE
ILLUSTRATIONS ADDITIONNELLES
DE JAN FAGERROOS, MIIKA SAKSI,
PABLO STEFFA ET JANI TOLIN
CLIENT : AMNESTY INTERNATIONAL
FINLANDE, 2003

FREEDOM OF SPEECH
POSTER
ADDITIONAL ILLUSTRATIONS BY
JAN FAGERROOS, MIIKA SAKSI,
PABLO STEFFA AND JANI TOLIN
CLIENT: AMNESTY INTERNATIONAL
FINLAND, 2003

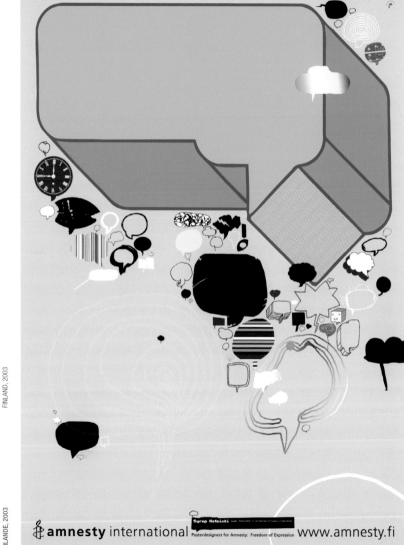

EVERYONE'S A VIP TO SOMEONE

EVERYONE'S A VIP TO SOMEONE
IMPRESSION SUR TEXTILE
CLIENT : GRAND MAGASIN STOCKMANN
FINLANDE, 2005

EVERYONE'S A VIP TO SOMEONE
PRINT DESIGN
CLIENT : STOCKMANN DEPARTMENT STORES
FINLAND, 2005

STOCKER GIRLS IDENTITY
POSTER
CLIENT: JIM & JILL
FINLAND, 2005

IDENTITÉ DE STOCKER GIRLS
AFFICHE
CLIENT : JIM & JILL
FINLANDE, 2005

BARBIE ROMANTIC REMIX
DÉTAIL D'UNE COLLECTION
D'IMPRESSION SUR TEXTILE
CLIENT : MATTEL INC.
ÉTATS-UNIS, 2005

BARBIE ROMANTIC REMIX
DETAIL FROM A PRINT DESIGN
COLLECTION
CLIENT: MATTEL INC.
USA, 2005

ROMANTIC

designergu8jsap / 069 / KOKORO & MOI

IDENTITÉ DU PROJET « IHME »
LOGOTYPE ET PUBLICITÉ
CLIENT : PRO ARTE FOUNDATION
FINLANDE, 2008

"IHME" PROJECT IDENTITY
LOGOTYPE AND ADVERTISEMENT
CLIENT: PRO ARTE FOUNDATION
FINLAND, 2008

Hei kaikki,

Mitä teille
kuuluu?
Tehdään jotain
yhdessä.

IHME-editio no:1

Tämä sivu on toteutettu Antony Gormleyn idean ponjalta. Hän on brittiläinen taiteilija, joka tulee toteuttamaan ensi vuonna TaideSäätiö Pro Arten kuraaoja yhtaiällisen teoksen Helsinkiin.

TaideSäätiö Pro Arten ensimmäinen tuotanto, IHME 8 - kansainvälisten nykytaiteilijoiden aiokuvia ja -ideoita -ohjelma esitetään Sio Meidalla lauantaina 29.7.2008 aivaen klo 17.00.

Lisätietoja Antony Gormleysta, IHME 8 - ohjelmasta ja TaideSäätiö Pro Artesta löydät osoitteesta www.proartefoundation.fi

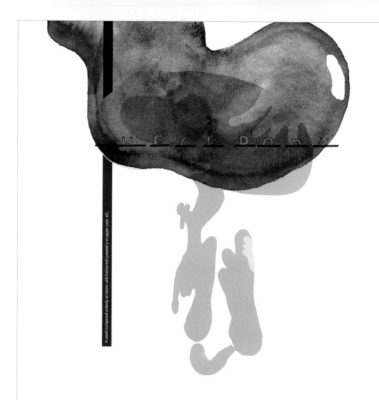

A word composed entirely of letters with horizontal symmetry in upper case. #2.

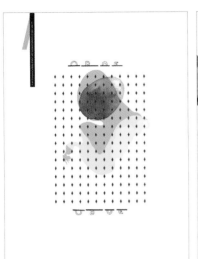

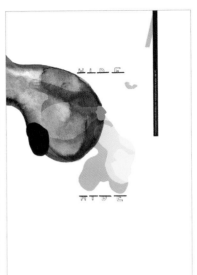

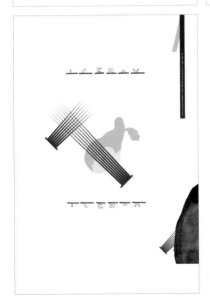

HORIZONTAL SYMMETRY
ILLUSTRATIONS
CLIENT : MAGAZINE *SUGO*
ITALIE, 2005

HORIZONTAL SYMMETRY
ILLUSTRATIONS
CLIENT: *SUGO* MAGAZINE
ITALY, 2005

1-0
IMPRESSION SUR TEXTILE
CLIENT : UNIQLO
JAPON, 2007

1-0
PRINT DESIGN
CLIENT : UNIQLO
JAPAN, 2007

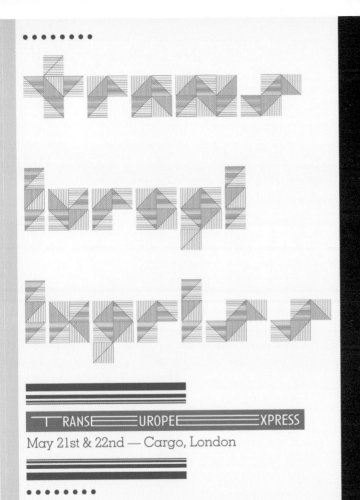

May 21st & 22nd — Cargo, London

IDENTITE DU FESTIVAL
« TRANS EUROPE EXPRESS »
FLYER
ROYAUME-UNI, 2004

IDENTITY OF THE "TRANS EUROPE
EXPRESS" FESTIVAL
FLYER
UK, 2004

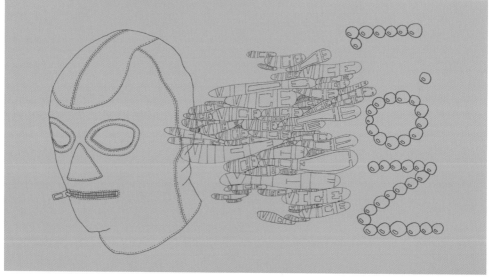

GUERRE
ILLUSTRATION
POUR L'OUVRAGE
GRAPHIC POETRY
ÉDITÉ PAR VICTIONARY
ROYAUME-UNI, 2005

WAR
ILLUSTRATION FOR
THE *GRAPHIC POETRY*
BOOK PUBLISHED
BY VICTIONARY
UK, 2005

INVITATION POUR
LE LANCEMENT
DU MAGAZINE
VICE SCANDINAVIE
SUÈDE, 2005

VICE SCANDINAVIA
LAUNCH CAMPAIGN
INVITATION
SWEDEN, 2005

IDENTITÉ DU CLUB
ULTIMO DISKO
AFFICHE
ROYAUME-UNI, 2005

ULTIMO DISKO CLUB IDENTITY
POSTER
UK, 2005

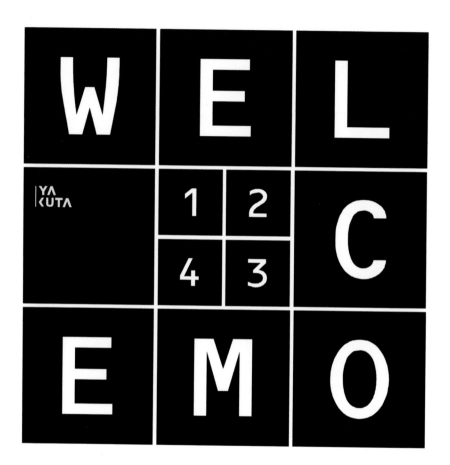

 Samples Sound On/Off

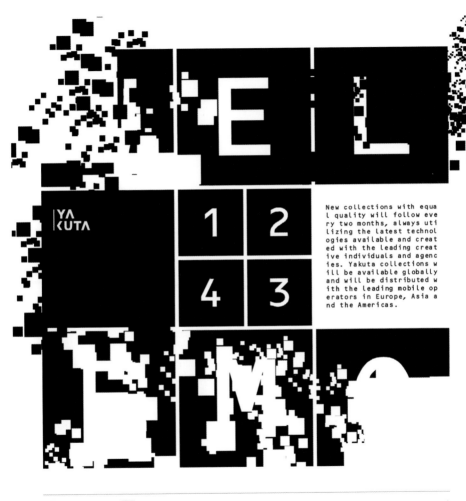

New collections with equal quality will follow every two months, always utilizing the latest technologies available and created with the leading creative individuals and agencies. Yakuta collections will be available globally and will be distributed with the leading mobile operators in Europe, Asia and the Americas.

> Samples   > Sound On/Off

PAGES PRÉCÉDENTES :
SITE INTERNET
DE YAKUTA
FINLANDE, 2001

PREVIOUS PAGES:
YAKUTA WEBSITE
FINLAND, 2001

GUTEN MORGAN GEIST
DETAIL D'UNE COLLECTION
D'IMPRESSIONS SUR TEXTILE
CLIENT : SAVCOR ONE TILES LTD
FINLANDE, 2004

GUTEN MORGAN GEIST
DETAIL FROM A PRINT
DESIGN COLLECTION
CLIENT: SAVCOR ONE TILES LTD.
FINLAND, 2004

15XKF

Kari Hotakainen

PUNAHUKKA

KOM
TEATTERI

CHARTE GRAPHIQUE ET SCÉNOGRAPHIE
DE L'EXPOSITION « 15XKF »
CLIENT : DESIGN FORUM FINLAND
FINLANDE, 2007

DESIGN AND SCENOGRAPHY
OF THE "15XKF" EXHIBIT
CLIENT: DESIGN FORUM FINLAND
FINLAND, 2007

IDENTITÉ DE LA PIÈCE
DE THÉÂTRE *PUNAHUKKA*
AFFICHE
CLIENT : KOM THEATRE
FINLANDE, 2006

IDENTITY OF THE "PUNAHUKKA" PIECE
POSTER
CLIENT: KOM THEATRE
FINLAND, 2006

S Y R U P   H E L S I N K I

DIVIDED WE STAND
ILLUSTRATION
CLIENT : MAGAZINE *NORD*
ALLEMAGNE, 2006

DIVIDED WE STAND
ILLUSTRATION
CLIENT: *NORD* MAGAZINE
GERMANY, 2006

PAGES SUIVANTES :
IDENTITÉ DE PORTAALI ARCHITECTS
DIVERS SUPPORTS IDENITIAIRES
FINLANDE, 2008

NEXT PAGES:
PORTAALI ARCHITECTS IDENTITY
VARIOUS IDENTITY MATERIAL
FINLAND, 2008

juha kämäräinen
arkkitehti safa
+358 44 535 9857
juha.kamarainen@portaali.eu

portaali arkkitehdit
jääkärinkatu 10 b 44
00150 helsinki, finland
www.portaali.eu

portaali arkkitehdit
jääkärinkatu 10 b 44
00150 helsinki, finland
tel +358 44 535 9857
contact@portaali.eu
www.portaali.eu

designer/partner
+358 40 572 1787
Design Office KOKO3 Ltd
Tallberginkatu 1/101, 00180 Helsinki 18, Finland
tel: +358 9 685 4643 fax: +358 9 6855 2066
email: aino.brandt@koko3.fi web: www.koko3.fi
kka Halminen
/partner
8 40 722 0336
Design Office KOKO3 Ltd
Tallberginkatu 1/101, 00180 Helsinki 18, Finland
tel: +358 9 685 4643 fax: +358 9 6855 2066
email: jukka.halminen@koko3.fi web: www.koko3.fi
ka Parkkinen
58 40 722 0335
arkkinen
40 722 0335

IDENTITÉ DE KOKO3
CARTES DE VISITE
ET SITE INTERNET
WWW.KOKO3.FI
FINLANDE, 2006

KOKO3 IDENTITY
BUSINESS CARDS
AND WEBSITE
WWW.KOKO3.FI
FINLAND, 2006

Kokoro & Moi

IDENTITÉ DE KOKORO & MOI
CARTE DE VISITE
FINLANDE, 2008

KOKORO & MOI IDENTITY
BUSINESS CARD
FINLAND, 2008

REMERCIEMENTS / ACKNOWLEDGEMENTS:

Jenna Sutela, Mikko Ryhänen, Jan Fagerroos, Linda Linko, Sofia Østerhus, Christoph Senn, Johanna Lundberg, Simona Nascimento Da Silva, Janne Piippo, Liv Wadström, Maja Zetterberg, Matti Kataja, Riku Pihlanto, Janne Norokytö, Timo Koro, Robin Gavin, Jakob & Robert et tout le monde à Syrup, KOKO3, Miika Saksi, Pablo Steffa, Freeman & CTRL, Päivi Grönqvist et toute l'équipe de Vallila Interior, Yugo Katayama et toute l'équipe d'Escalator Records, Beni & Crew de Jim & Jill, Design Forum Finland, Reala, Åbäke, Enric Godes et Bruno Selies de Vasava, Payman de chez Le Shop, Teemu Brunila, Giorgio Camuffo, Saila-Mari Kohtala, Laura Sarvilinna et les femmes de chez Huippu, Paola & Pirjo ainsi que toute l'équipe de Jollas, Eat & Joy, Oski de Bob Helsinki, Burt Pahkalah & Stupido Family et tous ceux avec qui nous avons été amenés à travailler.

Jenna Sutela, Mikko Ryhänen, Jan Fagerroos, Linda Linko, Sofia Østerhus, Christoph Senn, Johanna Lundberg, Simona Nascimento Da Silva, Janne Piippo, Liv Wadström, Maja Zetterberg, Matti Kataja, Riku Pihlanto, Janne Norokytö, Timo Koro, Robin Gavin, Jakob & Robert and everyone at Syrup, KOKO3, Miika Saksi, Pablo Steffa, Freeman & CTRL, Päivi Grönqvist and everyone at Vallila Interior, Yugo Katayama and all at Escalator Records, Beni & crew at Jim & Jill, Design Forum Finland, Reala, Åbäke, Enric Godes and Bruno Selies at Vasava, Payman at Le Shop, Teemu Brunila, Giorgio Camuffo, Saila-Mari Kohtala, Laura Sarvilinna and the ladies at Huippu, Paola & Pirjo + the Jollas crew, Eat & Joy, Oski at Bob Helsinki, Burt Pahkalah & Stupido Family and everyone we have ever worked with.